EVERYTHING IS GHOSTS

poems by

Tyler Robert Sheldon

Finishing Line Press
Georgetown, Kentucky

EVERYTHING IS GHOSTS

ACKNOWLEDGMENTS

Thanks also to the editors of the following publications who gave homes to
the following poems, sometimes in earlier versions:

Coal City Review—"Rocky Ford Bridge"
The Dead Mule School of Southern Literature—"The Truth Is We Were All
Afraid of Death"
Thorny Locust—"Jimmy Baca Comes to Town"
The Write Bridge Zine—"Millie"

With love to my family, and to all my college friends. Most of all to Alex, my
muse.

With gratitude to Amy Sage Webb Baza, Liz Burk, Anders Carlson-Wee,
Chen Chen, Toby Daspit, Faith Ellington, Harley Elliott, Martha Garner,
Dana Gioia, Kal Heck, Walter Klumpp, Ted Kooser, Michelle Kreamer, Dave
Leiker, Denise Low, Clare Martin, Deb and Terry Maxwell, Patrice Melnick,
Nonah Palmer, Kevin Rabas, Micah Romero, Jason Ryberg, Bessie and
Tommy Senette, Mel Storm, and Suzanne Wiltz.

Publisher: Leah Huete de Maines
Editor: Christen Kincaid
Cover Art: *The Bird Bridge: Crossing Over.* Copyright © 2023 by
        Dave Leiker
Author Photo: *Halloween 2023.* Copyright © 2023 by Tyler Robert Sheldon
Cover Design: Elizabeth Maines McCleavy

Order online: www.finishinglinepress.com
        also available on amazon.com

Author inquiries and mail orders:
Finishing Line Press
PO Box 1626
Georgetown, Kentucky 40324
USA

Contents

Legacy 1

First Night.. 2

Breakfast 3

The Professor.. 4

We Later Learned Where Things Went Wrong 5

Rachel.. 6

The Truth Is We Were All Afraid of Death 7

Houseguests 8

Glass 9

Deb's Metals Class.. 10

Rocky Ford Bridge.. 12

Ghost Hunters Visit the William Allen White Library 13

Old Cars, Cigars, and Ghosts.. 14

And Luckily We All Saw Morning 15

Jimmy Baca Comes to Town 16

Jazz Chords, Like Friendly Ghosts 17

It's Not Crazy If It's Real.. 18

Sunrise With the Artists 19

And Then Everything Was Different 20

Friday Night Question 21

Hauntology... 22

Despite 23

Millie 24

Creative Writing 25

Gwen 26

We Never Learned Her Name.. 27

Before America Faces the Corner in the Abandoned House

    in the Woods 28

So Many Ways You Cannot See 29

On Our Own.. 30

They're All Still Here 31

LEGACY

This is the city
that cradles the college
that holds the office

that my grandfather worked in
almost half a century back,
the city where my parents met,

the college of teachers,
the years unspooling
in the eyes of their memories

as I settle into the dorms
forty years into my
grandfather's future.

The road opens before me
and yawns like the mouth
of a bright, waiting ghost.

FIRST NIGHT

We decide you'll stay with me in this part of the building
after you see the shadow people in your dorm room, sifting
through the no-windows night-dark air like cartoon clouds of bees

and walking through the wall into the hallway just outside.
In that part of the dorm, the part you left, where your roommate
now in technicality only claimed the better half before we showed,

folks whisper about the ghosts, this building old enough,
they say, to have some, one a baller who still dribbles his way
through the tiled floors when everyone, or almost, lies asleep.

We squeeze together on my narrow bed, safer this way, nobody
    waiting
for us but ourselves, stirred to blind-filtered morning by the phone
    alarm,
the coffee pot waiting, the only ghosts imprisoned in our dreams.

BREAKFAST

JG, new friend, asks if he can bum a smoke as we stand
at the cafeteria entrance in the student union. Seven AM sun
drifts in around his face, frames his brown and curled hair, and
his hands twitch just slightly in his pockets as he smiles like a man
covering bad news, and I have to tell him no, that I don't carry
cigarettes, only smoking the kind with cloves because they remind me
of fall even when it's not. We stack our plates with waffles, he takes
a paper box of orange juice, I pour coffee and we grab a table
by the window where the pond looks back at us with its watery eyes,
dragonflies just dots along the surface beyond the glass. JG says
there weren't many cigarettes where he'd been before this either,
and he says he means his time here in college, not the cafeteria
in particular. When I ask him where he was before, he says
the institution, and I don't press him further. Later he comes up
to my dorm, an old archtop guitar in tow, and we jam a while,
taking breaks to tune and talk. The institution, he tells me, let him
keep his guitar. It wasn't really all that bad.

THE PROFESSOR

Now he strides to the front
of the room: this unaging teacher
in a Brooks Brothers suit
who once taught my parents, and
still here he stands, up four flights
of stairs just as quickly as breathing,
and in this first class all the books
hunker like paving stones on the tops
of our desks with the weight of a
world from before we all lived.

Here to read Chaucer, we open
our books, and he recites
like a prayer the first lines
of the pilgrims who walked like
the chosen to their holiest place.
He smiles as though he has met them
himself, and none of us ask, but
we wonder about how much
he's seen, his eyes on a road
we do not yet know.

WE LATER LEARNED WHERE THINGS WENT WRONG

Courtney, who would later make every single guy in the dorm jealous
by throwing herself into my arms on Halloween with nothing on
but one of those sexy police costumes, the trapezoidal cap askew
across her dirty blonde hair, found me on our first day of college,
her face ragged with tears, having just broken up messily with her
boyfriend of years and years too long. She made her hesitant way
into my room, with me already headed on bewildered feet
to grab some tissues, neither of us with any idea who the other was.

She sat with me on the edge of my bed, ladling out little bits
of just how tough it all was, and here she was in this big new place,
and I was the first friend she'd made, and as she edged the words
out into the air she fiddled with her hair, a nervous tic she'd keep
for years after that day, when—done with class—my girlfriend
came in to meet us, and when we'd all hit the bowling alley together,
Courtney spinning to the radio hits before her turn, full of a secret
we'd only learn in time. And gradually, everything seemed fine.

RACHEL

whom we've never seen before meets us on our way
up the handicap-accessible ramp outside the dorm,
hello-how-are-ya's like she's known us her whole life,
and out of her baggy jeans sticks the handle of a knife,
clip glimmering in the streetlight that pops staccato

above our heads. She takes one of our bags, full with
our weekend-trip clothes and care package miscellany,
and leads us both inside. Rachel turns around her baseball cap
like she's gotta catch 'em all. We all head down the hall,
and she motors on about her husband, one state south,

who knows she's here at college, but not her dorm room
number, and could we help her keep it that way, now
that we're all the best of friends. I tell her yes, of course,
see the bruises on her arms, don't ask. Rachel tells us she
knows everyone, and doles out her hellos, and something
in her eyes is haunted, dark green vessels full of ghosts.

THE TRUTH IS WE WERE ALL AFRAID OF DEATH

It didn't start off as a coherent plan, or some sort of destination
that we both wanted to end up at. It was late, we were a little bit
     wasted,
and there's only so many card games you can vodka-slog through
before things are just too much. It's really true. I'd gone fish enough,
and it was already like ten-thirty pm. What we needed was less
conversation, more tacos. Whoever left first, they kept bringing
up the ghost everyone talked of, living (dying? whatever) in the
room down the hall. Like the whole dorm knew about it, this person,
this b-baller, had died while dribbling, and you could still catch wind
of the *thump thumpa thump* if you were out late enough, then.
So maybe it was Rachel who got out first and tried to be creepy
about it—*we gotta make it before we hear the ball, gotta be sneaky.*
We kept bumping the wall, freaking ourselves out, thinking we'd
as soon find hell before finding the car, but we got there, and
     somebody
(maybe it was Jason) got us to Taco Bell. We took the interstate back,
paper wraps flapped across the floor, soft tacos and sauce like abstract
     art,
and we all felt lucky it was Jason's car, not ours. We munched
cinnamon twists and sipped Baja Blast, watching the lines of the night
     road
streak past. Then somehow, we all were back in the dorm, crawling
     back
down the hall, all our ears perked for the sound of the ball.

HOUSEGUESTS

Sammi, art major, lives in a big midwestern house down the street
from campus, the kind with two stories and enough rooms one could
live with their whole family and maybe bump into them twice a week
if that. Also, so she swears, the upstairs houses at least a few ghosts.
When we go over in the evenings, old video games blaring away
in the living room, and I have to make my way up there because
someone else is using the downstairs bathroom, I quickly flick on
every light, walk only along the edges of the hallway, and make it
just in time. I hear a creak, though everyone is still downstairs,
and I don't think about it, I do my very best, as I head back down.

GLASS

On break from class we head to the Art Annex,
down the hill from campus, and watch the blowers
spin their molten glass, bright like taffy, into shape.
This is best done in wintertime, when the wind
outside the tin-roofed building whistles like a
night-guard, and the furnace heat alleviates
one's cold-cramped back.

Chris spins a drinking glass, narrows its waist
with giant snips, clips it off, slides it
in the cabinet with its neighbors. Later
it will grow a crack, and he'll give it to me,
and it will overlook the pond outside the dorm,
the windowed morning bright like taffy
in the hand, almost more than we can stand.

DEB'S METALS CLASS

When I come to your art class
the brave teacher waits
for every one of us to settle in.
Her eyes hold the whole room,
Her whole face a bright smile,
her hand on a torch.

As you heat metal threads with the end of a torch,
I try to gather the way of this class:
this circlet of students arrayed like a smile,
the pieces of metal that lie there in wait,
the small cries of triumph that brighten the room.
Deb nods every time someone turns a piece in.

As I take all of the goings-on in,
the small hiss of gas from the mouth of each torch
lends a faint haze to the air in the room.
You hang back to talk for a bit after class.
As you gather your things, Deb happily waits,
and we both like her, and can't help but smile.

Deb asks us over, which isn't her style,
so we drive to her house and work our way in:
the whole yard a garden that breathingly waits,
each leaf and flower as bright as a torch.
She holds open the door and the three of us pass
into the cool, darkened living room.

Huge paintings line every wall of the room.
She introduces her husband, who gives us a smile
and shakes our hands fast;
his wheelchair barely holds his joy in.
Happy to meet up, his eyes gleam like a torch.
He asks how we like his paintings, and waits.

They tell us their story, and the evening gets late:
They'd met as students outside of a classroom.
Terry says he already felt like a torch
when they met, could thereafter do nothing but smile,
and against this new bond, polio couldn't win.
They gaze out the window. The sun breathes through the glass.

ROCKY FORD BRIDGE

Five miles outside Emporia, Kansas

One night we fold ourselves into Courtney's tiny car
and cruise down to the old bridge just outside of town,
where the Reverend Bird killed his wife to wed another,
throwing her riven body like a wish into the creek below.

Good luck will come, so everyone has told us, to the one
who walks across this bridge, and sees her pale and
bloodied face, her tattered dress, and does not falter, and
makes it all the way across. JG pries one foot, another,
from the back seat and onto the old wood slats, and steps,
and steps, and trips. He walks, we watch, we wait.

When he breaks into a run, we wonder at his pace, and
if he's seen her, but even later, in the dorm—the lights
all on, his face as pale as the ghost of Sandy Bird—
he will not meet our eyes or let free a single word.

GHOST HUNTERS VISIT THE WILLIAM ALLEN WHITE LIBRARY

"But she did not fall from the horse, nor was she riding fast."
—*Obituary for Mary White, The Emporia Gazette, 1921*

Thank you, dear library, for the crowd which presses
its goosebumped way into the corners of your lobby
this evening (someone notes it's a Tuesday, so thank you too
for changing it up from the usual empty-lobby night). Thank you

for these hosting these strange machines, which beep and spin
in the red light, the overheads off, lest we scare our subject away.
Thank you for these three folks who've come all the way from
Missouri to make contact with a poor girl tree-struck on horseback,
dead decades ahead of her time. Thank you for being a library,

where silence is sacred as saddles in summer, and when you close
your eyes to hear a bit better you might hear the rhythm of hooves.
Thank you for helping us picture her there, perhaps in the far corner,
tied to this place for eons to come, cowboy hat still askew.
Thank you for helping us see this night through.

OLD CARS, CIGARS, AND GHOSTS

Chris, related to at least one guy in the mafia,
tells us he's bringing Cuban cigars back from his trip
to the island this summer. How many do we want,
he asks. We don't smoke all that much, but we
say as many as you want to bring us, Chris, and
he nods. That's what they're best at, he says.
Old cars, cigars, and far too many ghosts.

AND LUCKILY WE ALL SAW MORNING

Chris pulls from his desk drawer a big bottle that used to hold his
    pills,
holds it to the light. Inside looks like all-green potpourri, smells
    nothing
like a plant, but Chris puts some in his pipe and lights it 'til it's red.

He gives us some, leans back, closes one eye, and then the other,
Until we leave he doesn't say a word. We take our bag and head
back to the dorms. Later you set a spark to this new stuff, say Hey,

it's great, then cough, and spit, and stumble 'til I get you on the bed.
You make it to the bathroom and so much later purge yourself
to safety. Chris they find the next day, sleeping until three,

Which he's never done before. We don't speak about this until
months later, the memory hazy, or so we say, our eyes averted,
everywhere but on each other. We all know he could be dead.

JIMMY BACA COMES TO TOWN

and in the little Irish pub across from our future
apartment (stumbling distance, we'll always say), faculty
and English majors lean in as the famous poet talks
about his book. Lindsey, bartender, passes my drink
across the bar, highball sweating, dark beer
floating atop pale cider. Magic in a glass,
you always said.
                          Jimmy sees we're rapt,
regales us in gravelly voice how he'd written
and read his way to freedom beyond, at last,
the system that had kept him down.
The cider sits under its ceiling of night-black ale,
waiting for its chance as I raise the glass
and take the first long drink.

JAZZ CHORDS, LIKE FRIENDLY GHOSTS
for Kevin Rabas

The building keeps changing. It leaves
traces of its life in every note we play,
my professor and I, riffing jazz
and reading poetry in what is for now
a pizza joint. Folks line the wall

and order pies, and Kevin snaps a few
licks with his brushes across the snare,
and I'm comping chords like Freddie Green
on my worn-out off-white Strat. We play out

Horace Silver, we jam over our own
poems. Listeners nod and tap their feet,
shake red peppers onto slices so it sounds
like they've got maracas keeping time.

In a few years this will be a print shop,
and everyone will wear their shirts.
Later I'll leave town and this night will
float along behind me like a ghost,
and when I come back the building
will stand empty, waiting for
someone to give it its next name.

Kevin signals for the last few bars, and I
land on Eb7, my index finger laid
across the neck. Ten years in the future
the lights are off inside this joint, and it's all
darkness and dust and boards on windows.
And we all keep changing. But tonight

folks clap, and we pack up the mics
and drums, I case up my guitar, and
we find a table, where you have already
ordered us a supreme, and the lights
are yellow and warm, and slowly
the background music filters in.

IT'S NOT CRAZY IF IT'S REAL

We find an archway outside the art building,
framing the sidewalk, the only way out.
Don't pass under it, even the professors say,
or you'll never graduate. We walk carefully
around the arch until we're done. And even
afterward. They might, we reason,
come for your degree.

SUNRISE WITH THE ARTISTS

The sun climbs hand over radiant hand
toward the lip of the sky. Deb makes us all
coffee, and Terry holds a new brush
in one folded hand, painting the air,

surely planning a piece. He remembers,
he tells us, driving a van
with the other *wheelchair kids*
and finding a hill, racing their way

down again and again. He gives us
a grin. *Things used to be easier,*
he tells us, then laughs, his eyes
torches lighting the ghosts of his past.

Deb makes her way in and hands all of us cups.
The birds gather outside, the sun almost up.

AND THEN EVERYTHING WAS DIFFERENT

Courtney, who seems so calm, comes clean one night
as we sit together in my dorm room. JG's on his guitar,
strumming out a nervous melody. Sammi sits with her
on the bed, and seeing tears, reaches out to pat her knee.
Courtney describes an accident, out cruising late one night,
the other driver looking everywhere but toward her car
as his semi ran the light. She can remember, so she says,
the time before, when math and other studies were easy.
Now we all take her hand, fetch the tissues, as Courtney
begins quietly to cry.

FRIDAY NIGHT QUESTION

if after downing one too many witchcraft-esque drinks / where the dark Irish beer floats atop the festive cider / in such a way that it reminds you of keeping / your head just barely above water / too far from the beach at night / if after that last one you don't head back / to your room with friends / and get a little too familiar / and kiss the wrong person / move your mouth over the wrong person's also mouth / and can't think of what to say / when the only right person has enough and leaves / and don't lay unsleeping until morning / and then fumble for an apology / and mean every last syllable / can you still avoid the pain / is it even still possible / of losing everything

HAUNTOLOGY

"Does the 'historical' person who is identified with the ghost properly belong to the present? Surely not."
—Peter Buse and Andrew Stott on Jacques Derrida

It hurts when they leave. It
Hurts when they leave. It hurts
When they leave. It hurts. When
They leave it hurts. When? They
Leave it. They hurt, leave. It hurts.

DESPITE

Do we refuse, all of us / to meet each others' eyes / at breakfast because we know / something has shifted, or / because what has shifted / is ourselves—and are we / maybe even comfortable, still, and / what will happen when I ask / you to let me up to get more / cereal, the shimmering flakes full / with their illusory promise: greatness, / three r's, the tiger smiling from out of the blue / so much darker than the sky, / milk drifting into the depths of the bowl, melting / everything on the way down

MILLIE

Sammi's dog, bigger than Sam is tall, is afraid like death
of pool noodles. When we knock, she lets us in, and Millie,
this mastiff one could saddle like a horse, sees us come in

and waits, locked in place by a single foam tube wedged
in the open door. She whines as though this simple toy
has threatened her family, or taken her treats, and later

she eats with one eye on the bowl, and one on the door,
feeling the noodle's spectral presence. We watch her
from the couch. When later we leave, Millie looks out

from under the foam, a finger curved above her like the
ghost of Christmas Yet to Come, and we tell her *no, we
cannot take you with us*, and we tell her, *be brave*, and pet

her head, and she somehow steels herself, and gazes
back at us with the courage of a thousand dogs.

CREATIVE WRITING

after Albert Goldbarth

Everything is ghosts. Kevin, creative
writing professor, passes out templates
for screenwriting—the slots for people

who say things to each other, behavior
locked in, scripted like a mixtape, waiting
for us to give them names. Poetry

is much the same, a record in rhyme
of someone's time that we transcribe
like record grooves. Everything is

ghosts, and everything is also music.
Everything is also stars, what gets left
behind when pure bright energy throws

itself, almost expired, out into the void.
As I say, music is like this too, record grooves
the tracings of those who were before us,

their lights sometimes gone out
before we see them, vaulted
over distances we cannot fathom,

their voices somewhere in the scratching
of the needle, which even while you
weren't listening found its patient way

to the center, to the record's very end.

GWEN

One night Courtney sneers across the dorm room floor,
smacks JG's hand away as he sits and braids her hair.
We can finally all talk, she says, and stands, and we
ask her what she means. *I'm not like the other one,*
she says, *but I protect her.* JG's eyes go wide, but
Courtney says, *It looks like she can trust you, and so
will I.* Her hands go in her pockets, her feet spread wide,
a stance that's anything but Courtney's own. *Call me
Gwen,* she tells us. *Try not to piss me off.* We
introduce ourselves. She keeps her eyes on all of us,
unblinking, for the remainder of the night.

WE NEVER LEARNED HER NAME

A woman died once in the library stacks,
and has waited there for years, jumping
out at anyone who takes a book from the
fourth floor: musty tomes of Shakespeare
plays, the hidebound editions in the back
corner, their owners also so long dead.

Rachel takes us there one weekend night,
and up the rickety elevator after the iron
bars slide shut. We head back into the
corner, and soon we see our breath.
Air drops its heat like clothing in the dark.
Rachel's white as paper, and says she hears a voice.

And so in just ten minutes we've had our fill of scares.
We trip over each other in our hurry for the stairs.

BEFORE AMERICA FACES THE CORNER IN THE
ABANDONED HOUSE IN THE WOODS

Emporia, Kansas, 2016

This is the feeling of carrying a soon-to-be-lost fragment of time
home with you from your college-town video store, a weathered
DVD case with cracks along the edge, split along its length
from the corners from the last dumbfuck to pick it up, and inside it
though you won't find this out until later sits the wrong movie,
a disk of *Casper* when all you wanted was something actually dark,
even the movie on the cover, but failing that at least something
    horrific
enough to make you feel, Heather Donahue in the woods with a
    camera
and another camera and also a map until Mike throws it into the
    river,
and for a moment you're lost just like them, afraid to close your eyes
in case you miss the signs, dolls made of crossed sticks or red
    octagons
at the edge of the street warning that soon someone in a woods-
    green
Chevy will come and eat you up and leave your shoes in someone
    else's
front yard tree, except you keep watching the road, and make it
soon enough back home, where you start the DVD player and the
    FBI
warning plays, and right on cue outside your window it begins to
    rain

SO MANY WAYS YOU CANNOT SEE

and one of them happens like this: you're
back in the dorms, visiting a friend. You walk
down the hall with her, freshly straightened
up with elation from the indie journal editor
who has told you just that day that he likes
what you've sent in, and the spots begin
to fill in your vision at the edges.

Because you haven't told your friend, she
doesn't know you can't quite see, and you
bump into the wall on the way to the icy
night outside. The spots grow larger, and you
continue to act as though they aren't there.
You don't know anything beyond the wall
of dread this brings. You stand at the edge

of the lake in front of the building you've
just left, the walk covered in ice, and you
have somehow not slipped ass end over
teakettle, as your grandfather used to say,
which you used in a poem your editor said
he liked. The lake is there, and you can't see it,
not quite yet, but the ice is there as always too—

the ice gives off its low hiss, like TV static
in the other room, and when the spots begin
to recede—ghosts pulling back into the walls
of the house from your dreams—behind where
they have left there is one bright scratch,
a small fingernail of January moon.

ON OUR OWN

Our first apartment is right behind a church
down the street from the university. We move
all of our belongings there, out of the dorms,

before the RA knows—this postage stamp place,
tiny in a subdivided house, one small square
of kitchen counter and one window frame peeling

slowly away from the outside, smoke drifting down
from neighbors we won't meet for days—yes, but
it's ours, and just across the street there sits a bar,

and once we've moved all the way in—scrubbed
the walls and steamed the carpets, folded clothes
and found some chairs—we go there and buy drinks.

We laugh we turn off the ringers on our phones, and
later, maybe stumbling slightly, we finally make it home.

THEY'RE ALL STILL HERE

If you wait long enough
you'll be there forever

If you don't believe it
just go into the hall

or the street once nighttime falls
and listen

TYLER ROBERT SHELDON is the author of six other poetry collections including *When to Ask for Rain* (Spartan Press, 2021), a Birdy Poetry Prize Finalist. He is Editor-in-Chief of *MockingHeart Review,* and his work has appeared in *Dialogue: The Interdisciplinary Journal of Pop Culture and Pedagogy, The Midwest Quarterly, The Los Angeles Review, Ninth Letter, Pleiades, Slant, Tinderbox Poetry Journal*, and other places. His research interests include poetry and poetics, comics studies, pedagogy, and World War II. A Pushcart Prize nominee and winner of the Charles E. Walton Essay Award, Sheldon earned his PhD at LSU, and his MFA at McNeese State University. He spends his days teaching, writing, playing guitar, and catering to the whims of his tortoiseshell cat Chai. View his work at TylerRobertSheldon.com.

www.ingramcontent.com/pod-product-compliance
Lightning Source LLC
Chambersburg PA
CBHW030052100426
42734CB00038B/1305